WANTED!
— FAMOUS OUTLAWS —
BONNIE AND CLYDE

NOTORIOUS OUTLAWS OF THE GREAT DEPRESSION

TIM COOKE

 Gareth Stevens
PUBLISHING

Please visit our website, **www.garethstevens.com**.
For a free color catalog of all our high-quality books,
call toll-free 1-800-542-2595 or fax 1-877-542-2596.

Library of Congress Cataloging-in-Publication Data

Cooke, Tim, 1961- author.
Bonnie and Clyde : notorious outlaws of the Great Depression / Tim Cooke.
    pages cm. — (Wanted! Famous outlaws)
Includes index.
ISBN 978-1-4824-4251-9 (pbk.)
ISBN 978-1-4824-4252-6 (6 pack)
ISBN 978-1-4824-4253-3 (library binding)
1. Barrow, Clyde, 1909-1934—Juvenile literature. 2. Parker, Bonnie, 1910-1934—Juvenile literature.
3. Criminals—United States—Biography—Juvenile literature. 4. Bank robberies—United States—History—20th
century—Juvenile literature. I. Title.
HV6785.C66 2016
364.15'52092273—dc23
[B]
                              2015027022

Published in 2016 by
Gareth Stevens Publishing
111 East 14th Street, Suite 349
New York, NY 10003

© 2016 Brown Bear Books Ltd

For Brown Bear Books Ltd:
Editorial Director: Lindsey Lowe
Managing Editor: Tim Cooke
Children's Publisher: Anne O'Daly
Design Manager: Keith Davis
Designer: Melissa Roskell
Picture Manager: Sophie Mortimer

Picture Credits: Front Cover: Library of Congress. Alamy: Everett Collection Historical 26, John Frost Newspapers 41;
Backgate: 30; Dallas Police Department: 8, 31; Dreamstime: Kathryn Sidenstricker 21; FBI: 17, 25, 28, 39, 45; Forgotten
Weapons: 9; IFCAR: 16; Library of Congress: 4,5, 7, 10, 11, 12, 20, 27, 33, 35; National Archives: 13, 18, 22, 23, 29, 44; Robert
Hunt Library: 42; Shutterstock: 4, Everett Historical 40; TexasHideout Tripod: 36, 37; Thinkstock: James Steidl 15;
Topfoto: AP 32, The Granger Collection 24, 34; Vanessa E. Zekowitz: 19; Warner Bros. Seven Arts: 43.

Brown Bear Books has made every attempt to contact the copyright holder. If anyone has any information please
contact licensing@brownbearbooks.co.uk

Manufactured in the United States of America
CPSIA compliance information: Batch #CW16GS. For further information contact Gareth Stevens, New York, New York at 1-800-542-2595.

108017

CONTENTS

INTRODUCTION

Bonnie Parker and Clyde Barrow were sweethearts and outlaws. They robbed banks, gas stations, and stores. They killed anyone who got in their way.

To begin with, some people thought Bonnie and Clyde were heroes. In the 1930s life in the United States was hard. There had been an economic crash. Firms closed and many people lost their jobs. People were poor. When Bonnie and Clyde started to rob banks many people thought they were fighting against poverty. That view of the outlaws soon changed. Bonnie and Clyde's gang shot dead at least nine police officers. They also killed

New Yorkers gather near the Stock Exchange on Wall Street in October 1929. They were worried about their savings.

civilians. People turned against them and the gang then spent most of its time on the run from the police.

Growing up in a boom

Bonnie and Clyde were teenagers in the 1920s. The United States experienced an **economic boom**. It was an exciting time. There were plenty of jobs. The country's wealth increased. Many Americans had money to buy new goods, such as radios and automobiles. Life for women changed dramatically. The symbol of the modern woman was the **flapper**. These young women had bobbed haircuts, wore shorter skirts, and were independent. Many also had jobs for the first time.

Economic boom A period when there is a lot of business activity and sales are high.

Flapper A fashionable young woman in the 1920s.

This sculpture in Washington, D.C., shows unemployed men standing in line waiting for food during the Great Depression.

The bust

The economic boom of the 1920s was too good to last. People and banks invested money in the **stock market**. In 1929, the stock market suddenly lost most of its value. The economy collapsed. People rushed to take their money out of the banks. By 1933, 4,000 banks had closed. Millions of people lost their life savings. Unemployment in the cities rocketed as companies went bust. Things were no better in the countryside. Large parts of the Midwest turned into a dust bowl. The soil dried up and blew away in the wind. Crops failed and families starved. Desperate people drifted across the country looking for work. The period was called the **Great Depression**.

Feeling of betrayal

Most Americans felt betrayed by the government. Many men had fought against the Germans in World War I (1914–1918). They came home from the war hoping for a secure future. They believed that if they worked hard and saved money, they would be able to live well. The Depression crushed their hopes. In the same way, many women had enjoyed being able to work in the 1920s. Now jobs were scarce, and women found themselves stuck at home again.

Bonnie Parker and Clyde Barrow were young adults when the Great Depression started. They faced difficult futures and made a choice. They decided to embark upon a life of crime.

Poor, unemployed men looking for work in the Great Depression walk past a billboard from the boom years that advises taking the train.

Stock market A place where people buy shares in companies in the hopes of making money.

Great Depression A long period of low global economic activity in the 1930s.

A Criminal Childhood

Clyde Barrow's early life was a struggle against poverty. He soon turned to crime to help make money.

Clyde Barrow was born on March 24, 1909, in Texas. His family was very poor. In the early 1920s they lived in West Dallas. At the time the neighborhood was a run-down area. The family had so little money they had to live under their station wagon while they saved to buy a tent.

Clyde's first incident with the law came when he was 17 years old. He rented a car and did not return it, so he was arrested. He found a number of jobs, but he began to steal cars and rob stores

Clyde carried an M1918 Browning Automatic Rifle. It had been designed for use by soldiers in World War I.

to add to his small wage. Clyde was arrested several times. In April 1930 he was sent to Eastham Prison Farm. Eastham had a **reputation** as being a tough, brutal place.

A hardened criminal

Clyde was released from jail in February 1932. He was no longer a minor criminal. He had become a murderer. While in jail, Clyde had killed his cellmate, "Big Ed" Crowder. Crowder had assaulted Clyde. Clyde smashed his skull with a lead pipe.

On his release, Clyde formed the Barrow Gang. They began robbing small grocery stores and gas stations. Clyde carried a Browning automatic rifle. He blamed the authorities at Eastham Prison for his mistreatment by Crowder and threatened to take revenge on the prison.

★ ★ ★
A CHANGED MAN

People who knew Clyde said his experiences in Eastham changed him. The guards did not protect him from Ed Crowder, who assaulted him often. When he was released, his sisters said his character had changed so much they barely recognized him. Another prisoner said he had become a "rattlesnake."

Reputation How someone or something is judged by the general public.

Focus: Texas Prison System

Texan prisons were known to be tough.
Eastham Prison Farm, where Clyde Barrow
was held, was one of the toughest.

A prison warden (right) and two guards inside a Texas prison in the early 20th century.

After the end of the Civil War (1861–1865) the Southern states that had joined the **Confederacy** suffered from a high level of crime. There was also a lack of money. In Texas, the state could not afford to keep all its criminals in prison. To solve the problem, the state government hired out prisoners to private companies as workers. The prisoners worked during the day in mines or on railroads or **plantations**.

Prison farms

The hiring out of prisoners was abolished in 1910. Instead, Texas started to buy their own plantations and farms. By 1921, state prison farms covered more than 81,000 acres (33 hectares). They did not make any money, but the state used the prison farms as a form of punishment. The Eastham Prison Farm in Huntsville, where Clyde Barrow was sent, was where Texas sent its toughest prisoners. They harvested cotton under the blazing Texan sun. It was hard, physical work.

African American prisoners working on a Texas prison farm in 1934.

LIFE IN THE PRISON

Conditions for prisoners on the prison farms were poor. The cells were filthy and full of rats and insects. The guards were tough and often treated the prisoners badly. Violence between the prisoners was common. The guards ignored unexplained deaths among the prisoners.

Confederacy The country set up by the Southern states that left the United States in 1861.

Plantation A large estate for growing crops.

The First Meeting

In January 1930 Bonnie and Clyde met in West Dallas. It was love at first sight, but they were soon separated.

Downtown Dallas pictured in around 1930. Bonnie and Clyde lived in West Dallas, which was a poorer part of the city.

Bonnie Parker was born on October 1, 1910, in Rowena, Texas. Her father died when she was four years old, and her mother took Bonnie and her brother and sister to live with their grandparents in a poor area of Dallas known as "Cement City." Today it is part of West Dallas.

By the time she met Clyde Barrow, Bonnie was already married. She had dropped out of school to marry Roy Thornton on September 25, 1926. She was only 15 years old. The marriage was not happy. The couple separated, although they never divorced. Thornton was later sent to prison for murder.

A talented poet

Bonnie worked as a waitress in a diner, but she lost her job. Lonely and sad after her failed marriage, she started to write poetry. At school, she had been talented at writing and had won several academic honors. Shortly after she met Clyde Barrow in 1930, he was sent to Eastham Prison Farm. Bonnie decided to wait for him. She dreamed of the **romantic** adventures they would share on his release.

A MODERN WOMAN?

Some historians think Bonnie is the real reason Bonnie and Clyde became so popular. They say that Clyde was a lazy, violent criminal. But they describe Bonnie as a tough, independent woman. She tried to make the best of her life and she always stood by Clyde in times of trouble.

Bonnie and Clyde lived as a married couple, even though Bonnie was already married.

Romantic Associated with an idealized and perfect view of reality.

Robbers and Killers

After leaving jail in February 1932, Clyde Barrow put together a gang. Bonnie joined his life of crime.

The small town of Stringtown was the scene of the Barrow Gang's first intentional murder.

Bonnie was soon in trouble. On April 19, 1932, the gang tried to rob a hardware store in Kaufman, Texas. The robbery went wrong. Bonnie and another member of the gang, Ralph Fults, were caught. Fults was tried and sent to prison. Bonnie spent a few months in the county jail. She was not **indicted**. Instead, she was freed and warned to stay out of trouble. She did not listen to the warning.

The Barrow Gang

The Barrow Gang may have committed their first murder on April 30, 1932. Storekeeper J. N. Bucher was killed accidentally after he had opened his safe for the gang. The next murder came in August 1932. Clyde was with gang members Raymond Hamilton and Ross Dyer. They went to a barn dance just over the Texas state line in Stringtown, Oklahoma. The three men were drinking beer when the local sheriff and his deputy approached them. Clyde and Hamilton fired on both men. Deputy Eugene Moore was killed. Sheriff C. G. Maxwell was seriously injured.

Another killing soon followed. This time the victim was Howard Hall. He was a storekeeper in Sherman, Texas. Clyde shot him dead while robbing the store. Hall was not quick enough to hand over the $28 (about $485 in today's money) he had in his cash register.

THE FORD MODEL V-8

The Barrow Gang stole cars to get around. Clyde was a skilled driver who could drive up to 1,000 miles (1,600 km) at a time. His favorite car was the Ford V-8, which was known for its comfort, speed, and good handling. Clyde is said to have written to carmaker Henry Ford praising the V-8.

Storekeeper Howard Hall was killed because Clyde thought he was too slow to hand over the money from his cash register.

Indicted Charged with a crime and ordered to go to court for trial.

Christmas Day murder

In December 1932, Clyde recruited a new member to his gang. William Daniel (W. D.) Jones was a family friend. He was only 16 years old at the time, and admired Clyde. On Christmas Eve, Jones left Dallas with Bonnie and Clyde.

The next day, they were in Temple, Texas. Clyde tried to steal a Model A Ford **Roadster**. The driver was Doyle Johnson. He was a new father on his way home for Christmas dinner with his young family. Johnson tried to stop Clyde from stealing his car but Clyde shot him dead.

Clyde's favorite car was the Ford Model V-8. Clyde liked to steal cars that were fast enough to outrun the police.

BEAUMONT 3715

BEAUMONT 3715

W. D. Jones quit the gang in September 1933. He said later that he'd had "enough blood."

Another killing

Two weeks later, Clyde shot and killed Deputy Sheriff Malcolm Davis in Tarrant County. The Barrow Gang had walked into a trap the deputy had set for a criminal friend of Clyde. The friend was thought to have carried out a bank robbery. The sheriff was waiting in the house when Clyde showed up and shot him. The gang was now wanted for killing five people.

YOUNG GANG MEMBER

W. D. Jones was part of the Barrow Gang from Christmas 1932 until September 1933. When he felt the police were closing in on the gang, he tried to quit. Clyde stopped him from leaving, but Jones eventually stole a car and escaped. He later served six years in prison for his part in the gang's crimes.

Roadster A sporty, open-top or convertible automobile with two seats.

The Family Gang

In March 1933 Clyde's brother Buck was released from jail. He joined the Barrow Gang with his wife, Blanche.

This photograph shows Buck and Blanche while on the run with the gang in 1933.

Marvin "Buck" Barrow had been sent to jail for robbery in November 1929. He escaped a few months later and went home to West Dallas. There he married his sweetheart, Blanche Caldwell. Blanche and some of Buck's family convinced him to return to jail and serve the rest of his **prison term**. Buck was released on March 22, 1933. He and Blanche met up with Bonnie and Clyde and joined the gang. The two couples and W. D. Jones moved to an apartment in Joplin, Missouri.

The gang ended up hiding from the law in the small town of Joplin, Missouri.

Odd neighbors

For two weeks they stayed inside. But their presence was soon noticed by people in the small local community. No one from the apartment went out during the day. People started to wonder who lived there. The gang began to play noisy card games and have parties. Beer had been illegal during the 1920s, but in March 1933 President Franklin D. Roosevelt had made it legal again. One night, during a particularly noisy party, Clyde accidentally fired his rifle. The neighbors contacted the Joplin police department.

BUCK AND BLANCHE

Blanche was an unlikely outlaw's wife. She fell in love with Buck before she knew he was a criminal and did her best to get him to give up his outlaw life. When she failed, she decided to join him. After Buck was released from jail, he was determined to meet up with Clyde. Blanche joined the gang, too.

Prison term The period for which a criminal is sent to prison.

Shootout in Joplin

Five policemen answered the call to the apartment in Joplin. They had no idea who was living there.

Joplin was to be the gang's last refuge. They spent the rest of their lives on the run.

On April 13, 1933, the police arrived in two cars and approached the apartment. They thought they were simply dealing with a group of noisy people at a drunken party. They called for everyone to come out of the building with their hands up. Instead Clyde and Buck Barrow, Bonnie, and W. D. Jones burst out firing Browning Automatic Rifles. Blanche did not shoot. Instead, she ran out of the building screaming. The police were so shocked and surprised that they did not shoot at her.

Going on the run

Better armed than the police, the gang shot their way out of the apartment building and past the police. Outside, Bonnie provided covering fire while

Clyde, Buck, and W. D. Jones jumped into their car. As they made their getaway, Jones was shot in his side. The gang drove off down the street to pick up Blanche. She had run off to catch her little white dog, who had escaped during the shooting.

Of the five police officers, two were killed and another was seriously injured. The incident became known as the Joplin **Massacre**. The Barrow Gang had become serious outlaws.

ARMING THE POLICE

In the 1920s and 1930s, outlaws such as John Dillinger and Clyde Barrow often used submachine guns or automatic rifles. The FBI (Federal Bureau of Investigation) and some police forces began to use the same weapons. They also used armored cars to fight the outlaws. However, most law enforcement agents only carried a shotgun. It was no match for the criminals' weapons.

The apartment still stands on Oakridge Drive in Joplin.

Gaining Publicity

The police searched the gang's apartment in Joplin. The things they found inspired the public's interest in Bonnie and Clyde.

Bonnie pretends to rob Clyde in this photo. It was on one of the rolls of film.

The apartment was full of personal possessions. These included Blanche and Buck's wedding certificate and Buck's prison **parole** papers. There was also a copy of a long poem by Bonnie called "Suicide Sal." Bonnie had written it while she was in jail in spring 1932. The poem told the story of a girl in jail who had been left by her gangster boyfriend. Bonnie's poem was published in many newspapers.

Caught on film

Also in the apartment were two used rolls of camera film. When the pictures were developed, they revealed some of the most

The Story of "Suicide Sal"
Bonnie & Clyde's Hideout

We each of us have a good "alibi"
For being down here in the "joint",
But few of them really are justified,
If you get right down to the point.
You have heard of a woman's "glory"
Being spent on a "downright cur",
Still you can't always judge the story
As true, being told by her.
As long as I stayed on that "Island"
And heard "confidence" tales from the "gals",
There was only one interesting & truthful,
It was the story of "Suicide Sal".
Now "Sal" was a "gal" of rare beauty,
Tho' her features were coarse & tough;
She never once faltered from "duty"
To play on the "up and up".
"Sal" told me this tale on the evening,
Before she was turned out "free"
And I'll do my best to relate it,

Bonnie wrote
her poem about
Suicide Sal
while she was
being held in
prison in 1932.

★★★ NATIONWIDE FAME

The newswire service
had been set up to
write news stories that
were sent to papers
around the country.
It helped to make the
Barrow Gang front-page
news far beyond Texas.
Readers were fascinated
by the photos of Bonnie
and Clyde and by
Bonnie's poem. The
couple were famous.

famous crime images of all time.
The pictures showed Bonnie and Clyde
holding weapons and posing for the camera.
They were probably taken by W. D. Jones.
In one photograph, Bonnie pretends to hold
up Clyde with a shotgun. In another, she has
her foot on a car bumper. She has a pistol on
her hip and a cigar in her mouth. Bonnie was said
not to like the picture. The poem and photographs
made Bonnie and Clyde famous. Everyone wanted
to read about them.

Parole When a prisoner is released before the end
of a prison term.

Focus: Public Heroes

For some Americans, Bonnie and Clyde were heroes. They were fighting against the authorities that people blamed for the Great Depression.

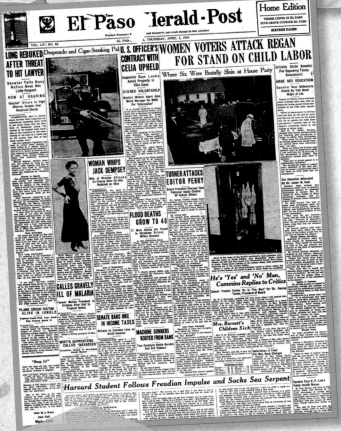

Photos of Bonnie and Clyde appear on the front page of a newspaper from El Paso, Texas.

The effects of the Great Depression left many Americans in poverty. By 1932 10 million people were out of work. Another 30 million people had very little money. Many turned to minor theft to try to raise money for food. Many of these people also followed the stories of more ambitious robbers.

Men such as "Babyface" Nelson and "Machine Gun" Kelly held up banks in towns throughout the Midwest. They were thieves and murderers, but the public loved to read about them. Many people **sympathized** with the criminals. They saw the outlaws as fighting against the authorities and the banks that had caused the Great Depression. The public thought they understood why criminals felt they had to follow a life of crime.

Crime in the Depression

The nature of crime had changed during the 1930s. Better highways and better maps made it possible for outlaws to travel easily. Criminals often targeted banks in small towns in the Midwest. These banks were not well guarded. Robbers could attack a bank and leave town before the police even knew about it.

★★★
CRIME FIGHTER

J. Edgar Hoover was director of the Federal Bureau of Investigation (FBI). He did not see criminals as public heroes. He called them public enemies. Hoover made catching famous criminals his priority. By 1935 FBI agents had killed or captured the most famous outlaws of the Great Depression.

George "Machine Gun" Kelly was an armed robber and kidnapper from Tennessee. He was also seen by many as a public hero.

Sympathized Understood someone else's feelings and behavior.

25

On the Run

With their photographs on the front page of every newspaper, it became harder for Bonnie and Clyde to stay out of public view.

WANTED FOR MURDER
JOPLIN, MISSOURI

26 U 00 6

CLYDE CHAMPION BARROW, age 24, 5'7", 130#, hair dark brown and wavy, eyes hazel, light complexion, home West Dallas, Texas. This man killed Detective Harry McGinnis and Constable J.W. Harryman in this city, April 13, 1933.

BONNIE PARKER   CLYDE BARROW

CLYDE BARROW

This man is dangerous and is known to have committed the following murders: Howard Hall, Sherman, Texas; J.N. Bucher, Hillsboro, Texas; a deputy sheriff at Atoka, Okla; deputy sheriff at West Dallas, Texas; also a man at Belden, Texas.

The above photos are kodaks taken by Barrow and his companions in various poses, and we believe they are better for identification than regular police pictures.

Wire or write any information to the

Police Department.

This police department WANTED poster used photographs taken by gang members.

The outlaws were on the run. They did not want to risk staying in tourist parks or motels where they might be recognized. Instead, they camped or slept in their cars. The gang stayed one step ahead of the police. Clyde stole a new car every week or two. They took their clothes to public laundries for cleaning. When they went to get their clothes, they checked for police activity. If there was any chance of being caught, they left the clothes and bought new ones.

Bonnie's accident

On June 10, 1933, Clyde was driving fast on a deserted highway through a region of Texas called the Panhandle. He ignored signs that a bridge was out and had to swerve at the last minute. The car crashed down a steep **embankment**. Clyde and W. D. Jones escaped. Bonnie was trapped inside the car, which burst into flames.

Bonnie's screams alerted two local farmers. They managed to pull her from the burning car. They took her to a farm to treat her injuries. A suspicious farmer called the sheriff. The outlaws were forced to flee. They took the sheriff and a deputy hostage but later released them unharmed in Oklahoma.

BONNIE'S INJURIES

Bonnie was seriously injured in the car fire. Her right leg was so badly burned the bone was visible. She almost died from her injuries. For weeks she was half conscious. After she recovered, her leg was permanently damaged. Walking became difficult for her.

A freight train passes beside a highway in the Texas Panhandle.

Embankment A bank of earth that carries a road or railroad over low ground.

Shootout at the Motel

While Bonnie recovered from her injuries, the gang decided to stay at the Red Crown Tourist Court in Platte City, Missouri. It was a big mistake.

Bonnie was seriously hurt. The gang wanted to give her time to recover, so they broke their own rule and took her to a motel. They rented two brick cabins joined by garages. The locals were suspicious of the new arrivals. Blanche only registered three guests, but the motel owner saw five people going into the cabins. The gang paid for everything with coins. They also taped newspapers over the windows of the cabins.

Toward midnight that evening, July 20, 1933, the local police and **reinforcements** from Kansas City surrounded the cabins. A gunfight began as the gang ran to their getaway car. Clyde had to carry Bonnie to the car, because she was unconscious from her injuries. Buck was hit in the head and badly wounded.

Another narrow escape

A police car blocked the gang's path. W. D. Jones fired at it until the driver was forced to pull out of the way. The police continued firing as the gang sped off. Bullets shattered the car windows. **Shards** of glass flew into Blanche's eyes, badly damaging them. For the outlaws, life on the run was becoming even harder.

DEATH OF BUCK

The shootout at Red Crown was a turning point for the gang. Buck Barrow died a few days later from his injuries after another police shootout at an old amusement park in Iowa. Blanche was arrested as she cradled her dying husband. She spent six years in jail. Later, she wrote about her time with the gang.

Blanche is arrested after the shootout with police in Iowa. She was jailed for attempted murder.

Reinforcements Extra personnel who increase the numbers of a force.

Shards Sharp-edged pieces of glass, rock, or metal.

Eastham **Breakout**

Clyde Barrow was unusual among outlaws. As well as breaking out of prison, he also broke into prison to free his friend Raymond Hamilton.

Clyde had wanted to take revenge on Eastham Prison Farm since his imprisonment in 1932.

For two months after the shootout at the Red Crown Tourist Court, the gang went into hiding again. Clyde was finally ready to carry out his threat to attack Eastham Prison Farm. He hid two **revolvers** at the edge of the farm's land. Early on January 16, 1934, Hamilton was working near the farm boundary. He and an **accomplice** named Joe Palmer found the hidden guns. They shot their two guards and escaped. One of the guards later died.

A full car

Clyde was waiting for Hamilton and Palmer with a getaway car. To Clyde's surprise, three other criminals also joined them. Clyde drove for

OKLAHOMA STATE PENITENTIARY

Institution — OKLAHOMA STATE PENITENTIARY   Location at — McALESTER, OKLAHOMA.

Received 10-3-3?
From Ottawa Co.
Crime Murder
Sentence Death yrs. mos. days
Date of sentence
Sentence begins 10-3-35
Sentence expires Death
Good time sentence expires 12-30-3?
Date of birth Occupation G.L.
Birthplace Lr. Nationality
Age 24 Com Mod.
Height 56½ Eyes Blue
Weight 165 Hair Bro.
Build Mod.

Scars and marks

CRIMINAL HISTORY

NAME	NUMBER	CITY OR INSTITUTION	DATE	CHARGE	DISPOSITION OR SENTENCE
No. S.P. 65949					
Henry Methvin	O-61	Ottawa Co.	10-9-34.	S.K.Rel	to Sheriff 3-14-35.

2-21-31 State Pen.,Huntsville,Texas#65949 as Henry Methvin; from Refugio Co.,Theft & Aslt.to Murder-10 yrs. Escaped 1-16-34.

(Please furnish additional history and police record on separate sheet.)

This criminal record card for Henry Methvin was created at the Oklahoma State Penitentiary in 1935.

★ ★ ★

HENRY METHVIN

Henry Methvin was serving ten years in prison for robbery. After he escaped with Hamilton and the others, he joined the Barrow Gang. He committed murders with Clyde. His father later helped the police trap Bonnie and Clyde. No one knows if Henry also helped to give away his friends.

250 miles (400 km), then dropped off two of the men. The third, Henry Methvin, joined the Barrow Gang, along with Hamilton and Palmer.

The prison guard who died was named Major Crowson. After his death, the governor of the Texas prisons, Lee Simmons, became determined to destroy the Barrow Gang. He knew just the man for the job.

Revolvers Pistols with a revolving chamber to hold bullets.

Accomplice A person who helps someone commit a crime.

Frank A. Hamer

The man chosen by Lee Simmons to track down Bonnie and Clyde was a former Texas Ranger, Frank A. Hamer.

Frank A. Hamer (left) discusses plans to catch the outlaws with two other law enforcement officials.

Hamer had a legendary reputation for catching criminals. His career had started early in the 20th century. Hamer was almost 50 years old when Simmons hired him to hunt down the Barrow Gang. The pay was half what Hamer was earning as an officer in the Texas Highway Patrol, but Hamer took the pay cut to take the job. He was eager to catch the outlaws who had so far **outwitted** the law.

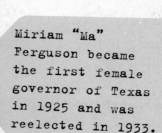
Miriam "Ma" Ferguson became the first female governor of Texas in 1925 and was reelected in 1933.

MIRIAM "MA" FERGUSON

Lee Simmons was worried that Hamer would not be allowed to hunt the outlaws. The appointment had to be approved by the Texas governor, "Ma" Ferguson. Ferguson was thought to be soft on crime. She had pardoned more than 100 prisoners during her second term. In this case, however, Ferguson allowed Hamer to have the job. She wanted Bonnie and Clyde caught.

Cat and mouse

Hamer decided the best way to catch Clyde was to try to understand how his mind worked. For 102 days, Hamer followed reports of Clyde's movements from the police. He figured out exactly how the gang moved around. He realized that they traveled in a circle around the Midwest. Clyde crossed in and out of states. That took advantage of the fact that state law forces were not allowed to cross into other states. Hamer figured out that the gang had base cities such as Dallas, Texas, and Joplin, Missouri. They carried out their robberies from these different bases.

Outwitted Got the better of someone by outsmarting them.

Focus: Texas Rangers

Frank A. Hamer was a former Texas Ranger. The Rangers were famous for being one of the toughest law enforcement agencies in the country.

Texas Rangers on patrol for the Union Army during the Civil War (1861-1865).

The Rangers were first formed in 1823. They protected American settlers in what was still the Mexican territory of Texas. At the start of the Texas Revolution in 1835, when the settlers rebelled against the Mexican government, the Texas Rangers became law enforcers for the state. They guarded the frontier during the fighting that led to Texan independence in 1836.

After Texas joined the United States in 1845, the Rangers remained the main law enforcers in Texas. They patrolled the border and fought Native

Americans. They also chased outlaws. In 1877 the Rangers caught the outlaw John Wesley Hardin, who had killed 42 people.

The Rangers were civilians. They supplied their own horses and weapons. In remote parts of state, the Rangers were known to take the law into their own hands. By the 1930s, many Texans thought the Rangers were too violent. Frank A. Hamer, for example, had killed at least 80 people. The state started to turn the Rangers into a more **conventional** police force.

★★★

"ONE RIOT, ONE RANGER"

This famous saying is associated with the Texas Rangers after Ranger Captain "Bill" McDonald was sent to Dallas in 1896 to stop an illegal boxing fight. When asked where his backup was, he is alleged to have said there was only one fight so only one Ranger was needed.

This statue of a Ranger stands outside the Texas Ranger Museum in Waco, Texas.

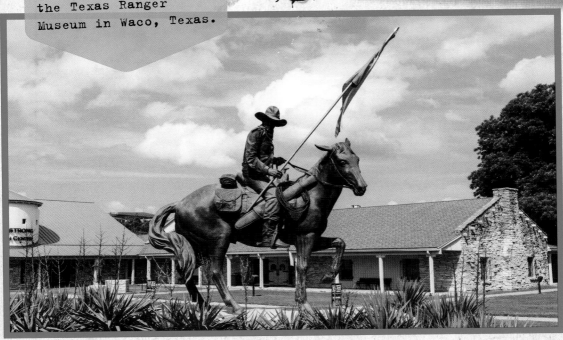

Conventional Operating in a more normal or traditional way.

Grapevine Killings

Any public sympathy for the Barrow Gang disappeared after the Grapevine Killings of Easter Sunday in 1934.

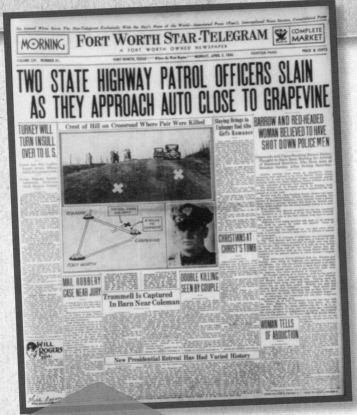

FORT WORTH STAR-TELEGRAM

TWO STATE HIGHWAY PATROL OFFICERS SLAIN AS THEY APPROACH AUTO CLOSE TO GRAPEVINE

On April 1, 1934, near Grapevine, Texas, the gang were approached by two highway patrolmen. Henry Methvin began firing at them and Clyde Barrow joined in. Troopers Edward Wheeler and H. D. Murphy were killed. Methvin later claimed that Bonnie had taken part in the shootings. He said she had stood laughing over the bodies. This was not true, but the public believed it. Public outrage grew when Murphy's fiancée went to his funeral in her wedding dress. The Highway Patrol and the Texas governor's office offered a combined reward of $2,000 for the bodies of the Barrow Gang.

A price on their heads

Five days after the Grapevine murders, Clyde and Methvin killed 60-year-old police constable Cal Campbell outside Commerce, Oklahoma.

The gang also **kidnapped** the town's police chief, Percy Boyd. They later released him unharmed. Boyd had seen Campbell's murder. He had not learned Methvin's name but he gave the authorities evidence to issue **warrants** for the arrest of Clyde Barrow and Bonnie Parker. Time was running out for them.

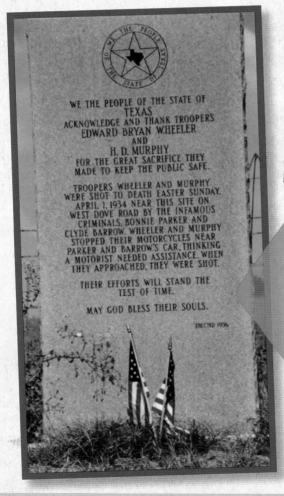

WE THE PEOPLE OF THE STATE OF
TEXAS
ACKNOWLEDGE AND THANK TROOPERS
EDWARD BRYAN WHEELER
AND
H. D. MURPHY
FOR THE GREAT SACRIFICE THEY
MADE TO KEEP THE PUBLIC SAFE.

TROOPERS WHEELER AND MURPHY
WERE SHOT TO DEATH EASTER SUNDAY,
APRIL 1, 1934 NEAR THIS SITE ON
WEST DOVE ROAD BY THE INFAMOUS
CRIMINALS, BONNIE PARKER AND
CLYDE BARROW. WHEELER AND MURPHY
STOPPED THEIR MOTORCYCLES NEAR
PARKER AND BARROW'S CAR, THINKING
A MOTORIST NEEDED ASSISTANCE. WHEN
THEY APPROACHED, THEY WERE SHOT.

THEIR EFFORTS WILL STAND THE
TEST OF TIME.

MAY GOD BLESS THEIR SOULS.

ERECTED 1996

This memorial to the two dead troopers stands on the site of the Grapevine killings.

Kidnapped Seized and held someone against their will.

Warrants Documents authorizing the police to make an arrest.

Closing In

After studying the gang for 102 days, Hamer was ready to make his move. He knew where they were heading next.

Frank A. Hamer (front, right) chose his posse himself so he knew he could trust them.

Hamer had worked out that the gang moved in a circular pattern along state lines to avoid capture. He also knew they visited their families regularly. He figured out that their next visit was likely to be to Henry Methvin's family in Louisiana.

Betrayed

Hamer got ready to make his move. He ordered a large number of Browning Automatic Rifles. He also ordered 20 **rounds** of armor-piercing bullets. He handpicked a **posse** of five men. On May 21, the posse left Texas for Shreveport, Louisiana. There they waited until they got word that the gang was nearby.

Clyde, Bonnie, and Henry Methvin had agreed that they would meet on an isolated highway in Bienville, Louisiana, close to Methvin's family home. Methvin's father, Ivan, had done a deal with Hamer. He told the posse where the outlaws would be and when they were expected to arrive. In return, Hamer promised that Henry Methvin would be spared the death sentence if he was captured. Everything was ready for the final shootout.

> This car is parked on the isolated road where the outlaws arranged to meet.

★★★ THE POSSE

Hamer's posse included two men who could identify Bonnie and Clyde. Ted Hinton knew Bonnie from her waitressing days, and Bob Alcorn knew Clyde by sight. The other members of the posse were former Texas Ranger Manny Gaul, Sheriff Henderson Jordan from Bienville, Louisiana, and deputy Prentiss Oakley.

Rounds Individual bullets fired by a gun.

Posse A group of citizens helping a sheriff.

Fatal Ambush

Early on the morning of May 23, 1934, the posse was waiting as a car approached it at top speed.

This photograph shows the car riddled with bullet holes after the attack.

There were two people inside the car. Clyde Barrow was driving. Bonnie Parker was in the passenger seat. As Clyde sped along the isolated road, he saw Ivan Methvin's truck blocking his path. The truck seemed to have broken down. The posse was hidden in the woods along the side of the road waiting to **ambush** Bonnie and Clyde.

Shot dead!

What happened next is uncertain. According to some accounts, the posse opened fire as Clyde slowed down to pass the truck. Other accounts

A Dallas newspaper reports the killings. Newspaper sales rose steeply.

state that one of the posse ordered the car to stop. The rest of the posse then opened fire. The firing continued until the posse had emptied 150 rounds into the car. Clyde and Bonnie were both struck many times and killed. Hamer did not want to give them any chance to escape. He made sure no one could have survived before ordering the attack to stop. Henry Methvin had escaped the ambush. He had hitchhiked to his father's home in the previous days.

★★★ FAMILY REUNIONS

Bonnie and Clyde made sure they visited their families regularly. Bonnie, in particular, missed her mom and liked to visit. The outlaws' mothers urged them to surrender many times. After Bonnie and Clyde died, their mothers were both found guilty of helping them. They were each sentenced to 30 days in jail.

Ambush A surprise attack made by people from hidden positions.

Focus: Bonnie and Clyde's Legacy

Bonnie and Clyde were only just dead when curious members of the public flocked to the small town of Arcadia to try to see their bodies.

The car in which Bonnie and Clyde died became a tourist attraction in Arcadia.

By dusk on the day of the killings, the population of the small Louisiana town had risen from 3,000 to 12,000. The roads into town were blocked. Everyone wanted to see the famous outlaws. They cut off pieces of their hair and clothes as **souvenirs**.

Separated forever

Bonnie and Clyde had separate funerals. They had asked to be buried together, but the Parker family would not allow this. Bonnie's funeral became a public event. The funeral home was filled with floral tributes. It was said that other outlaws such as the criminals John Dillinger and "Pretty Boy" Floyd sent flowers. The biggest floral arrangement came from the Dallas newspapers. Bonnie's death had helped to increase the number of papers they sold to half a million a day. The newspapers printed another poem by Bonnie, called "The Trail's End."

Since their deaths in 1934, Bonnie and Clyde have been the subject of books and movies. The most famous movie, *Bonnie and Clyde*, was made in 1967. It made the outlaws' lives on the run seem more romantic than they had ever really been.

"THE TRAIL'S END"

This is the beginning of Bonnie's poem. She saw the gang as being in the tradition of other outlaws.

You've read the story of Jesse James
of how he lived and died.
If you're still in need;
of something to read,
here's the story of Bonnie and Clyde.

Now Bonnie and Clyde are the Barrow gang
I'm sure you all have read.
how they rob and steal;
and those who squeal,
are usually found dying or dead.

The 1967 movie suggested that outlaws lived exciting and romantic lives.

Souvenirs Things that are kept as reminders of people, places, or events.

ROGUES' GALLERY

As poverty became widespread during the Depression, some criminals who stepped outside the law became household names.

"Ma" Barker
(1873–1935)

Ma Barker's real name was Arizona Barker. She was the mother of several criminals who formed the Barker Gang. Ma Barker ran the gang, which carried out robberies and kidnappings across the Midwest. She was killed in a shootout with the Federal Bureau of Investigation (FBI).

"Pretty Boy" Floyd
(1904–1934)

Charles Arthur Floyd was a bank robber. He got his nickname because he looked young. His gang killed up to 10 police officers. Floyd was popular, however. People saw him as a victim of the Depression. He was shot dead by law enforcement officials.

John Dillinger
(1903–1934)

John Dillinger became the FBI's Public Enemy Number One in June 1934. His gang robbed 24 banks. He was said to be very violent, although he was only known to have killed one police officer. Dillinger was on the run for a year before he was shot dead by FBI agents as he was leaving a movie theater in Chicago.

"Baby Face" Nelson
(1908–1934)

George Nelson got his nickname because of his small size and young appearance. He was a bank robber who worked with John Dillinger. Nelson was responsible for killing a number of policemen. The FBI shot him dead.

"Machine Gun" Kelly
(1895–1954)

George Francis Kelly got his nickname from his favorite weapon, the Thompson submachine gun. He was an armed robber. His biggest crime was the kidnapping of a businessman in 1933. Kelly was paid a ransom of $200,000. He was caught that same year and spent the rest of his life in jail.

GLOSSARY

Accomplice A person who helps someone commit a crime.

Ambush A surprise attack made by people from hidden positions.

Confederacy The country set up by the Southern states that left the United States in 1861.

Conventional Operating in a more normal or traditional way.

Economic boom A period when there is a lot of business activity and sales are high.

Embankment A bank of earth that carries a road or railroad over low ground.

Flapper A fashionable young woman in the 1920s.

Great Depression A long period of low global economic activity in the 1930s.

Indicted Charged with a crime and ordered to go to court.

Kidnapped Seized and held someone against their will.

Massacre The indiscriminate killing of many people.

Notoriety Fame gained by bad or evil actions.

Outwitted Got the better of someone by outsmarting them.

Parole The release of a prisoner early for good behavior.

Plantation A large estate for growing crops.

Posse A group of citizens helping a sheriff.

Prison term The period for which a criminal is sent to prison.

Reinforcements Extra personnel who increase the numbers of a force.

Reputation How someone or something is judged by the general public.

Revolvers Pistols with a revolving chamber to hold bullets.

Roadster A sporty, open-top or convertible automobile with two seats.

Romantic Associated with an idealized and perfect view of reality.

Rounds Individual bullets fired by a gun.

Shards Sharp-edged pieces of glass, rock, or metal.

Souvenirs Things that are kept as reminders of people, places, or events.

Stock market A place where people buy shares in companies in the hopes of making money.

Sympathized Understood someone else's feelings and behavior.

Warrants Documents authorizing the police to make an arrest.

FURTHER RESOURCES

Books

Crewe, Sabrina. *A History of the FBI.* The FBI Story. Broomall, PA: Mason Crest, 2009.

George, Linda, and Charles George. *The Great Depression.* Understanding American History. San Diego, CA: Referencepoint Press, 2012.

McNeese, Tim. *The Great Depression 1929–1938.* Discovering U.S. History. New York: Chelsea House Publishers, 2010.

Newton, Michael. *The Texas Rangers.* Law Enforcement Agencies. New York: Chelsea House Publishers, 2010.

Websites

https://www.fbi.gov/about-us/history/famous-cases/bonnie-and-clyde
Bonnie and Clyde's crimes and the story of the campaign to stop them from the website of the Federal Bureau of Investigation.

http://www.biography.com/people/bonnie-parker-9542045
A biography of Bonnie Parker from Biography.com, with a video.

http://www.biography.com/people/clyde-barrow-229532
The Biography.com page and video about Clyde Barrow.

http://www.roadsideamerica.com/map/theme/94
An interactive map of sites associated with Bonnie and Clyde, including where they carried out their crimes, with links to various museums and markers.

http://www.cinetropic.com/janeloisemorris/commentary/bonn&clyde/wdjones.html
A reprinted version of an interview given by W. D. Jones in 1968 about his life with Bonnie and Clyde.

Publisher's note to educators and parents: Our editors have carefully reviewed these websites to ensure that they are suitable for students. Many websites change frequently, however, and we cannot guarantee that a site's future contents will continue to meet our high standards of quality and educational value. Be advised that students should be closely supervised whenever they access the Internet.

INDEX